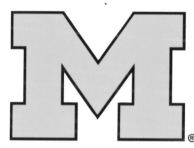

IS FOR MICHIGAN FOOTBALL

Celebrating the Tradition of Michigan Football

GREG NELSON

Ann Arbor
University of Michigan Press

Dedication

Thanks to my family—Lori, Erik, Marisa, Drew, Jacob, and Analise, as well as our parents—and friends, not only for their love and support, but for their constant encouragement and well wishes. And thanks to God for giving me the courage to turn my dreams into reality.

Special thanks to Steve Nelson for his boundless efforts and assistance and to Kelly Sippell for believing in the project from Day One: I appreciate your thoughts, ideas, energy, enthusiasm, and love for Michigan football.

Finally, thanks to the entire Wolverines football family—the many who have made Michigan football such a proud tradition to celebrate. Go Blue.

Copyright © by the University of Michigan 2009
All rights reserved
Published in the United States of America
The University of Michigan Press
Manufactured in the United States of America

⊗ Printed on acid-free paper

ISBN-13: 978-0-472-03387-4

2012   2011   2010   2009   4   3   2   1

Cover photo by Per Kjeldsen.

M is for Michigan Football

This is the story of a unique and remarkable football program. It's about a university, a community, and 129 years of history. It's about a team that has provided indelible moments, seemingly frozen in time, and extraordinary memories forever etched in the minds and emotions of fans. It's about victors and conquering heroes. This is the tale of a program so rich in pride and tradition that a story can be found within every letter of the alphabet. Yet all these stories can be represented by a single block letter: **M is for Michigan Football!**

is for Ann Arbor

Each September more than 100,000 people dressed in maize and blue descend upon Ann Arbor. Located in the heart of southeastern Michigan and home to Michigan football since 1879, Ann Arbor was originally named by John Allen, one of the city's founders, in honor of his wife, Ann. The accompanying word *Arbour* was added for the countless trees that dot the area. In 2009, Forbes.com named Ann Arbor the "Top College Sports Town" in America based on the Wolverines' all-around sports excellence and fan loyalty and Ann Arbor's top-flight restaurants and bars, cultural events (a symphony, a ballet, museums, concert halls), low crime rate, and affordable housing.

B is for Bo

A passionate, inspirational, and fiery leader, Bo Schembechler's legendary tenure as head coach of the Wolverines left an indelible mark on Michigan football. While his 234-65-8 record and 13 Big Ten championships place him among the elite coaches in college football history, Bo's commitment to excellence and love for the Maize and Blue will always remain at the heart of the Wolverine's success.

Glenn Edward "Bo" Schembechler
April 1, 1929–November 17, 2006

C is for Colors

Michigan colors its success Maize and Blue. In 1867, a committee of Michigan students was appointed to recommend emblematic colors for the University. Although the exact colors were initially difficult to define, maize was designed to represent a soft yellow—the color of the summer's finest "filled with sunshine" sweet corn. The selection of azure blue and maize became official on February 12, 1867. Today, those same maize and blue colors continue to represent a pride and passion that can be seen throughout Michigan Stadium™ on game days—from the field and sidelines to the grandstands, tailgate parties, and beyond. Go Blue!™

D is for Dominance

Michigan's historic football tradition has been built on a foundation of excellence and dominance that stretches back more than a century. A winning combination of outstanding players, innovative coaches, the highest academic and athletic standards, and teamwork has resulted in:

- 11 national championships
- 42 Big Ten championships
- 126 first-team All-Americans
- 3 Heisman Trophy winners

And still counting!

E is for Excitement

From intriguing cross-sectional match-ups and captivating Big Ten conference showdowns to impassioned rivalries against traditional foes like Michigan State, Notre Dame, Ohio State, and Wisconsin, there's no shortage of game-day excitement at Michigan Stadium.

Michigan's all-time record against its top rivals (through 2008 season):

67-29-5 vs. Michigan State
20-15-1 vs. Notre Dame
57-42-6 vs. Ohio State
49-12-1 vs. Wisconsin

11

F is for Ford

Gerald R. Ford, the 38th President of the United States, was a tremendous leader for the Michigan Wolverines. The two-way star played both center and linebacker at Michigan from 1932–1934 and helped the Wolverines to undefeated seasons and national championship titles in 1932 and 1933. The university retired his #48 jersey in 1994.

Michigan's retired uniform numbers:

11 Francis (1931–1934), Albert (1940–1942), and Alvin (1947–1949) Wistert
47 Bennie Oosterbaan (1925–1927)
48 Gerald Ford (1932–1934)
67 Ron Kramer (1954–1956)
98 Tom Harmon (1938–1940)

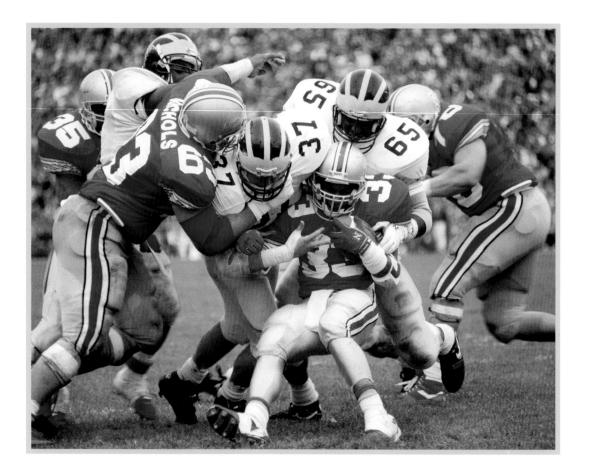

G is for *the* Game

Michigan vs. Ohio State is considered by many to be the greatest rivalry in college football and possibly all of sports. This annual showdown has determined the Big Ten champion more than 20 times, including a string of 10 consecutive years now known as the 10-Year War (1969–1978). Although the teams have lined up every year since 1918, the series gained prominence following the Wolverines' stunning 24-14 "upset of the century" in 1969 over the previously unbeaten Buckeyes. For many Michigan fans, that game is considered the most memorable, significant, and historic game in Michigan football history. It is *the* Game.

is for the Heisman Trophy

Originally awarded in 1935 as the Downtown Athletic Club (Manhattan) Trophy and later renamed the Heisman Memorial Trophy, this illustrious honor remains the most prestigious individual award in college football. Presented annually to the game's most outstanding player, 20 Wolverines have finished among the top 10 vote-getters and three Michigan standouts have captured the esteemed award.

Michigan's Heisman Trophy winners:

Tom Harmon, 1940

Desmond Howard, 1991

Charles Woodson, 1997

I is for *"there's no I in team"*

Coach Bo Schembechler said it best in this 1983 pep talk:

*"We want the Big Ten championship, and we're going to win it as a team. They can throw out all those great backs and great quarterbacks and great defensive players through the country and in this conference, but there's going to be one team that plays solely as a team. No man is more important than the team; no coach is more important than the team. **The team, the team, the team!"***

J is for the Jug

The Little Brown Jug is the world's most coveted water bottle. Coach Fielding Yost's Michigan teams had won 28 straight games prior to a 1903 showdown at Minnesota. Fearing fans might contaminate his team's water, Yost had a five-gallon jug purchased for 30¢ from a local store. After a dramatic 6-6 tie, the jug was left behind. Later, when Yost requested it back, Minnesota replied, "We have your little brown jug; if you want it, you'll have to win it."

Michigan leads in the trophy series 66-22-3 (through the 2008 season)

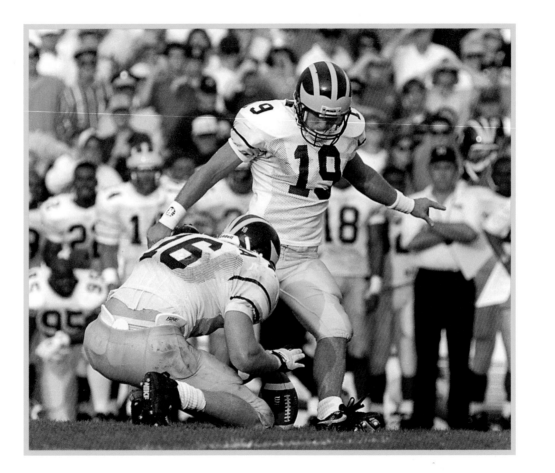

is for Kicking

Clutch field goals and electrifying kick and punt returns have all contributed to Michigan victories. From punters like Hayden Epstein and Adam Finley to kickers like Jay Feely, Mike Gillette, and Garrett Rivas, special teams have provided many extra special moments including Remy Hamilton's game-winning field goal against Notre Dame in 1994. Memorable and exciting punt returns by Desmond Howard in 1991 (93 yards) and Charles Woodson in 1997 (78 yards), both against Ohio State, set up both players to win the Heisman Trophy.

L is for Legacy

Bo Schembechler began his storied 20-year tenure as head coach at Michigan with a rallying cry to his players: *"Those who stay will be champions!"* This slogan foreshadowed the challenges Michigan football players would endure from the dramatic culture change initiated by Schembechler, who emphasized toughness and conditioning. More important, those words foreshadowed the success that would soon follow. Today, this slogan remains a team legacy, immortalized by a sign in the Michigan locker room and recognized as a lynchpin of the tradition of Michigan football.

M is for Michigan!

Founded in 1817, the University of Michigan is the state's oldest university and is internationally recognized for its academic excellence. With more than 40,000 students and 450,000 living alumni, the university generates top leaders in all areas of academic study. This tradition of excellence goes beyond the classroom to the playing field where the Wolverines have sent hundreds of players on to successful careers in the National Football League.

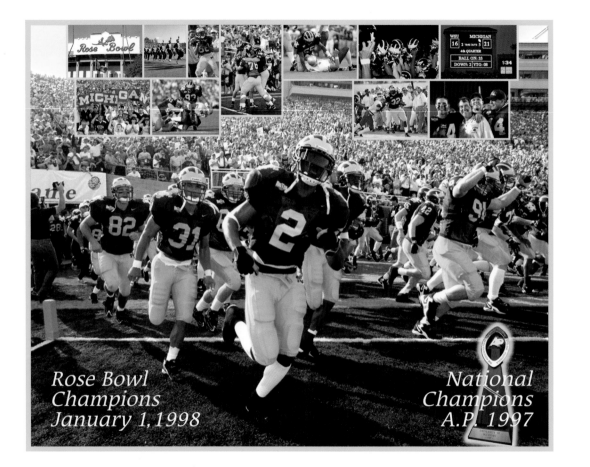

Rose Bowl
Champions
January 1, 1998

National
Champions
A.P. 1997

is for National Champions

Michigan's stirring 21-16 victory over Washington State University in the 1998 Rose Bowl capped a perfect 12-0 season and marked the program's 11th national collegiate football championship. The victory was highlighted by an aggressive defense, Chris Howard's 70 yards of rushing, Tai Street's two touchdown receptions, and quarterback Brian Griese's MVP performance: 18 completions for 251 yards and 3 touchdowns.

Hail, hail to Michigan!

National Championships:
1901, 1902, 1903, 1904, 1918, 1923, 1932, 1933, 1947, 1948, 1997

O is for One

With 872 victories, Michigan ranks #1 in all-time wins and #1 in all-time winning percentage (through 2008) in college football.

Jersey #1 is a coveted uniform, immortalized by record-shattering receiver Anthony Carter. From a 78-yard punt return in his first game to his thrilling game-ending touchdown catch and run to beat Indiana, A.C. was a three-time, first-team All-American and ranks among the greatest receivers in college and NFL history. Other standout receivers at Michigan who earned the right to wear the #1 jersey include Derrick Alexander, Braylon Edwards, and David Terrell.

P is for the Paul Bunyan Trophy

There's no question that Michigan shares an intense rivalry with in-state adversary Michigan State University. The battle for state bragging rights has been played annually since 1910 (with the exception of 1943–1944 due to WWII). Since 1953, the winner has been awarded the Paul Bunyan Governor of Michigan Trophy. Named after the giant, mythical lumberjack, the 4-foot-high wooden statue on a 5-foot base highlights Michigan's history as a lumber-producing state.

Michigan leads the trophy series 34-20-2 (through the 2008 season)

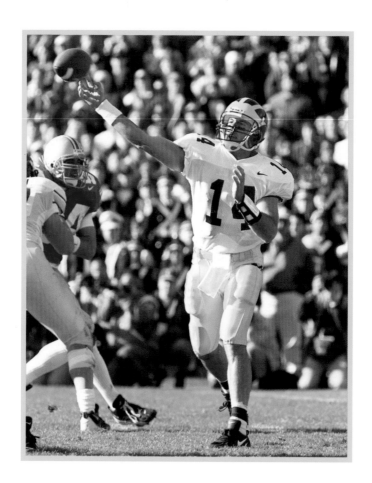

Q is for Quarterback

Few positions reflect the tradition of a football program like quarterback. Michigan's rich history has long been highlighted by outstanding signal callers such as the legendary Tom Harmon, Bob Chappuis, Chuck Ortmann, Bob Timberlake, Dennis Franklin, and Rick Leach. While Michigan's quarterbacks have managed several different offense types over the years (option attacks, pro-style set, a spread offense), one thing remains constant: the Wolverines continue to send a steady stream of signal callers to the NFL, including two-time Super Bowl MVP Tom Brady, Todd Collins, Elvis Grbac, Brian Griese, Jim Harbaugh, and Chad Henne.

R is for Roses

Michigan's annual quest for success is to reach the "Grand Daddy of All Bowl Games." First played in 1902, the Rose Bowl is the oldest and best attended bowl game in college football history. Michigan's 49-0 victory over Stanford in the inaugural Rose Bowl, a 49-0 win over USC in the first televised Rose Bowl in 1948, and the 21-16 national championship win over Washington State in 1998 rank among the special memories provided by Michigan's 20 Rose Bowl appearances.

S is for Michigan Stadium™

Originally built in 1927 for $950,000, Michigan Stadium™ is nicknamed "The Big House.®" Every home game for more than three decades has been played before at least 100,000 fans—a streak that began Nov. 8, 1975, with a 45-0 victory over Purdue. Official stadium capacity includes one extra seat "reserved" in eternity by Fielding Yost for former athletic director Fritz Crisler.

Top crowds in Michigan Stadium history (through the 2008 season):

112,118*—11/22/03 vs. Ohio State (100th meeting between UM-OSU)

111,726 — 09/13/03 vs. Notre Dame

111,609 — 10/30/04 vs. Michigan State

*Largest crowd in NCAA college football history

T is for the Tunnel

As fans wait in eager anticipation, a sea of maize and blue helmets emerges from the dark tunnel in the center of Michigan Stadium. Suddenly, a stream of Wolverine's players race from the tunnel to midfield where they jump and touch the Go Blue banner that has been a game day spectacle since the Homecoming game against Illinois in 1962. The banner, now supported by the M Club, was initially represented by a simple yellow Block M on a 6-foot-wide strip of fabric.

U is for Ufer

The energetic and enthusiastic radio voice of "Meeechigan" football for 37 years, Bob Ufer (1920–1981) remains an iconic member of Michigan's Athletic Hall of Honor. An outstanding track and field athlete at Michigan, Ufer is best remembered for his exuberant and highly partisan broadcasting style. His unique "Uferisms" included referring to Michigan as "Meeechigan" and honking on his "George Patton Schembechler" horn—the actual horn from U.S. General George Patton's Jeep—whenever Michigan scored.

V is for Victors Valiant™

"The Victors™," the Wolverine's fight song, was originally composed by Michigan student Louis Elbel following a last-minute victory over the University of Chicago that clinched a Big Ten title in 1898. John Philip Sousa called Elbel's composition "the greatest college fight song ever written."

Hail! to the victors valiant
Hail! to the conqu'ring heroes
Hail! Hail! to Michigan
The leaders and best!
Hail! to the victors valiant
Hail! to the conqu'ring heroes
Hail! Hail! to Michigan
The champions of the West!

is for Winged Helmet

One of the most widely recognized and intimidating icons in sports, Michigan's famed winged helmet remains a true symbol of Michigan football. The unique "winged" design dates back to 1938 when Coach Herbert O. "Fritz" Crisler first arrived from Princeton to begin a new era in Michigan football. An innovative offensive coach whose imaginative formations helped rack up yardage and points, Crisler developed the special helmet design to assist Michigan's quarterbacks in distinguishing Wolverine receivers downfield.

is for X's and O's

X's and O's are traditionally used by football coaches to signify the formations of offensive and defensive players. Michigan's long list of distinguished and innovative coaches rank among the best tacticians in history. From the "point a minute" teams of the early 1900s and Schembechler's "3 yards and a cloud of dust" style to the high-flying pro-sets and stretch-the-field spread offenses, Michigan's coaches have always kept opposing defenses on their heels.

Michigan coaching greats:

Fielding H. Yost: 165-29-10 (56 games without a loss, 6 national championships)
Harry G. Kipke: 46-26-4 (34-1-3 streak, 2 national championships)
Herbert O. Crisler: 71-16-3 (1 national championship)
Bennie G. Oosterbann: 63-33-4 (1 national championship)
Bo Schembechler: 194-48-5 (17 bowl games, 13 Big Ten championships)
Lloyd Carr: 122-40-0 (1 national championship)

is for Yost

Fielding H. Yost was Michigan's legendary coach, innovator, pioneer, and visionary. In 25 years of coaching, Yost won 6 national championships. His "point-a-minute" teams played 56 consecutive games without a loss from 1901–1905, outscoring their opponents 2,821 to 42. As Director of Athletics, Yost conceived the development of Michigan's athletic campus, including construction of Michigan Stadium, the university's golf course, the nation's first Intramural Sports Building, and the nation's first multipurpose fieldhouse, now aptly named Yost Ice Arena.

Z is for Zero

Zero was the number of points given up and the number of losses suffered by the 1901 Wolverines in an undefeated, untied, and unscored-upon perfect season.

Led by Fielding Yost, the Wolverines finished 11-0, outscoring the opposition 550-0, including a 128-0 win over Buffalo and a 49-0 win over Stanford in the first Rose Bowl. Stanford requested to "quit" after Michigan scored 32 third-quarter points in a game so lopsided that the Rose Bowl was not played again for 15 years.

M is for Michigan Memories

University of Michigan football fans are among the most loyal, knowledgeable, and passionate fans anywhere. Everyone who has ever watched the Maize and Blue in action has his or her own special memories: a mesmerizing play, a favorite player, an unforgettable game, or a game-changing performance.

Opinions and memories are recounted annually and passed from generation to generation. While those vivid recollections may differ from one fan to the next, one thing is certain—new magical moments happen each season, new heroes are discovered, and new champions are crowned.

What's your favorite recent Michigan football memory? (1968–2008)

Some options are presented on the following pages. Debate with friends and other UM fans; cast your votes at *www.press.umich.edu/survey/football.html*.

Most Memorable Game

- 24–12 upset of Ohio State (1969)
- 10–10 tie with Ohio State (1973)
- 21–16 national championship victory over Washington State (1998 Rose Bowl)
- 45–37 triple overtime victory over Michigan State (2004)

Greatest Single Game Performance

- Ron Johnson: Michigan record 347 yards and 5 rushing TDs vs. Wisconsin (1968)
- Tyrone Wheatley: 235 yards (1991 Rose Bowl)
- Tim Biakabutuka: 313 yards rushing vs. Ohio State (1995)
- Charles Woodson: punt return TD, interception in end zone, 37-yard reception vs. Ohio State (1997)
- Chris Perry: 51 carries vs. Michigan State (2003)

Best Comeback Victory

• Michigan	18 (1995)	• Michigan	45 (2004)	
Virginia	17	Michigan State	37	
• Michigan	28 (1997)	• Michigan	27 (2005)	
Iowa	24	Penn State	25	
• Michigan	38 (2003)			
Minnesota	35			

Best Single Catch

- Anthony Carter's game-winning TD vs. Indiana (1979)
- Desmond Howard's 4th down TD vs. Notre Dame (1991)
- Charles Woodson's one-handed interception vs. MSU (1997)
- Braylon Edwards' game-winning TD in triple overtime vs. MSU (2004)
- Mario Manningham's game-winning TD as time expired vs. Penn State (2005)

Best Receiver

- Anthony Carter (1979–1982): 161 receptions, 3,076 yards, 37 TDs
- Tai Streets (1996–1998): 144 receptions, 2,284 yards, 19 TDs
- David Terrell (1998–2000): 152 receptions, 2,317 yards, 24 TDs
- Marquise Walker (1998–2001): 176 receptions, 2,269 yards, 17 TDs
- Braylon Edwards (2001–2004): 252 receptions, 3,541 yards, 39 TDs

Best Quarterback

- Rick Leach (1975–1978): 48 career TD passes; 3-1 vs. OSU; 0 bowl wins
- Elvis Grbac (1989–1992): 71 career TD passes; 2-1 vs. OSU; 2 bowl wins
- Brian Griese (1995–1997): 33 career TD passes; 2-0 vs. OSU; 2 bowl wins; 1 national championship
- Tom Brady (1998–1999): 35 career TD passes; 1-1 vs. OSU; 2 bowl wins
- Chad Henne (2004–2007): 87 career TD passes; 0-4 vs. OSU; 1 bowl win

Best Running Back

- Ron Johnson (1966–1968): 2,440 career rushing yards
- Jamie Morris (1984–1987): 4,393 career rushing yards
- Tyrone Wheatley (1991–1994): 4,178 career rushing yards
- Anthony Thomas (1997–2000): 4,472 career rushing yards
- Mike Hart (2004–2007): 5,040 career rushing yards

Best Offensive Lineman

- Dan Dierdorf (1968–1970): consensus All-American, twice All–Big Ten
- John "Jumbo" Elliott (1984–1987): two-time All-American
- Jon Jansen (1995–1998): started 50 games, All-American, two-time co-captain
- Steve Hutchinson (1997–2000): 45 starts, did not allow a sack in final 2 seasons
- Jake Long (2004–2007): zero penalties and only one sack allowed in 2007, two-time All-American, two-time All–Big Ten

Best Special Teams Play

- Mike Lantry's 50-yard field goal, the first in Michigan history (1973)
- Desmond Howard's 93-yard punt return vs. OSU (1991)
- Remy Hamilton's 42-yard last-second field goal to beat Notre Dame (1994)
- DeWayne Patmon's tackle of Tim Dwight on kickoff return vs. Iowa to keep undefeated season alive (1997)
- Charles Woodson's 78-yard punt return vs. OSU (1997)

Best Defensive Player

- Ron Simpkins (1976–1979): 516 career tackles, 29 tackles for loss, 7 fumble recoveries
- Mark Messner (1985–1988): 36 sacks, 70 career tackles for loss
- Steve Morrison (1990–1994): 360 career tackles, 23 tackles vs. Illinois in 1992
- Charles Woodson (1995–1997): 18 career interceptions, 30 pass breakups
- Leon Hall (2003–2006): 45 tackles in 2006, 12 interceptions, 43 pass breakups

University of Michigan Wolverines, Football Season Records since 1969

1969 **Big Ten Champions**	1970	1971 **Big Ten Champions**	1972 **Big Ten Champions**
Coach: Glenn E. "Bo" Schembechler	**Coach:** Glenn E. "Bo" Schembechler	**Coach:** Glenn E. "Bo" Schembechler	**Coach:** Glenn E. "Bo" Schembechler
Season Record: 8-3	**Season Record:** 9-1	**Season Record:** 11-1	**Season Record:** 10-1
Conference Record: 6-1 (1st Place tie)	**Conference Record:** 6-1 (2nd Place tie)	**Conference Record:** 8-0 (1st Place)	**Conference Record:** 7-1 (1st Place tie)
Sept. 20 Vanderbilt W, 42-14 Sept. 27 Washington W, 45-7 Oct. 4 Missouri L, 17-40 Oct. 11 Purdue W, 31-20 Oct. 18 at MSU L, 12-23 Oct. 25 at Minnesota W, 35-9 Nov. 1 Wisconsin W, 35-7 Nov. 8 at Illinois W, 57-0 Nov. 15 at Iowa W, 51-6 Nov. 22 Ohio State W, 24-12 *Jan. 1 USC L, 3-10 *Rose Bowl, Pasadena, California	Sept. 19 Arizona W, 20-9 Sept. 26 at Wash. W, 17-3 Oct. 3 Texas A&M W, 14-10 Oct. 10 at Purdue W, 29-0 Oct. 17 MSU W, 34-20 Oct. 24 Minnesota W, 39-13 Oct. 31 at Wisconsin W, 29-15 Nov. 7 Illinois W, 42-0 Nov. 14 Iowa W, 55-0 Nov. 21 at Ohio State L, 9-20	Sept. 11 at NW W, 21-6 Sept. 18 Virginia W, 56-0 Sept. 25 UCLA W, 38-0 Oct. 2 Navy W, 46-0 Oct. 9 at MSU W, 24-13 Oct. 16 Illinois W, 35-6 Oct. 23 at Minnesota W, 35-7 Oct. 30 Indiana W, 61-7 Nov. 6 Iowa W, 63-7 Nov. 13 at Purdue W, 20-17 Nov. 20 Ohio State W, 10-7 *Jan. 1 Stanford L, 12-13 *Rose Bowl, Pasadena, California	Sept. 16 Northwestern W, 7-0 Sept. 23 at UCLA W, 26-9 Sept. 30 Tulane W, 41-7 Oct. 7 Navy W, 35-7 Oct. 14 MSU W, 10-0 Oct. 21 at Illinois W, 31-7 Oct. 28 Minnesota W, 42-0 Nov. 4 at Indiana W, 21-7 Nov. 11 at Iowa W, 31-0 Nov. 18 Purdue W, 9-6 Nov. 25 at Ohio State L, 11-14

1973 **Big Ten Champions**	1974 **Big Ten Champions**	1975	1976 **Big Ten Champions**
Coach: Glenn E. "Bo" Schembechler	**Coach:** Glenn E. "Bo" Schembechler	**Coach:** Glenn E. "Bo" Schembechler	**Coach:** Glenn E. "Bo" Schembechler
Season Record: 10-0-1	**Season Record:** 10-1	**Season Record:** 8-2-2	**Season Record:** 10-2
Conference Record: 7-0-1 (1st Place tie)	**Conference Record:** 7-1 (1st Place tie)	**Conference Record:** 7-1 (2nd Place)	**Conference Record:** 7-1 (1st Place tie)
Sept. 15 at Iowa W, 31-7 Sept. 22 Stanford W, 47-10 Sept. 29 Navy W, 14-0 Oct. 6 Oregon W, 24-0 Oct. 13 at MSU W, 31-0 Oct. 20 Wisconsin W, 35-6 Oct. 27 at Minnesota W, 34-7 Nov. 3 Indiana W, 49-13 Nov. 10 Illinois W, 21-6 Nov. 17 at Purdue W, 34-9 Nov. 24 Ohio State T, 10-10	Sept. 14 Iowa W, 24-7 Sept. 21 Colorado W, 31-0 Sept. 28 Navy W, 52-0 Oct. 5 at Stanford W, 27-16 Oct. 12 MSU W, 21-7 Oct. 19 at Wisconsin W, 24-20 Oct. 26 Minnesota W, 49-0 Nov. 2 at Indiana W, 21-7 Nov. 9 at Illinois W, 14-6 Nov. 16 Purdue W, 51-0 Nov. 23 at Ohio State L, 10-12	Sept. 13 at Wisconsin W, 23-6 Sept. 20 Stanford T, 19-19 Sept. 27 Baylor T, 14-14 Oct. 4 Missouri W, 31-7 Oct. 11 at MSU W, 16-6 Oct. 18 Northwestern W, 69-0 Oct. 25 Indiana W, 55-7 Nov. 1 at Minnesota W, 28-21 Nov. 8 Purdue W, 28-0 Nov. 15 at Illinois W, 21-15 Nov. 22 Ohio State L, 14-21 *Jan. 1 Oklahoma L, 6-14 *Orange Bowl, Miami, Florida	Sept. 11 Wisconsin W, 40-27 Sept. 18 Stanford W, 51-0 Sept. 25 Navy W, 70-14 Oct. 2 Wake Forest W, 31-0 Oct. 9 MSU W, 42-10 Oct. 16 at NW W, 38-7 Oct. 23 at Indiana W, 35-0 Oct. 30 Minnesota W, 45-0 Nov. 6 at Purdue L, 14-16 Nov. 13 Illinois W, 38-7 Nov. 20 at Ohio State W, 22-0 *Jan. 1 USC L, 6-14 *Rose Bowl, Pasadena, California

1977 **Big Ten Champions**	1978 **Big Ten Champions**	1979	1980 **Big Ten Champions**
Coach: Glenn E. "Bo" Schembechler	**Coach:** Glenn E. "Bo" Schembechler	**Coach:** Glenn E. "Bo" Schembechler	**Coach:** Glenn E. "Bo" Schembechler
Season Record: 10-2	**Season Record:** 10-2	**Season Record:** 8-4	**Season Record:** 10-2
Conference Record: 7-1 (1st Place tie)	**Conference Record:** 7-1 (1st Place tie)	**Conference Record:** 6-2 (3rd Place)	**Conference Record:** 8-0 (1st Place)
Sept. 10 at Illinois W, 37-9 Sept. 17 Duke W, 21-9 Sept. 24 Navy W, 14-7 Oct. 1 Texas A&M W, 41-3 Oct. 8 at MSU W, 24-14 Oct. 15 Wisconsin W, 56-0 Oct. 22 at Minnesota L, 0-16 Oct. 29 Iowa W, 23-6 Nov. 5 NW W, 63-20 Nov. 12 at Purdue W, 40-7 Nov. 19 Ohio State W, 14-6 *Jan. 2 Washington L, 20-27 *Rose Bowl, Pasadena, California	Sept. 16 Illinois W, 31-0 Sept. 23 at ND W, 28-14 Sept. 30 Duke W, 52-0 Oct. 7 Arizona W, 21-17 Oct. 14 MSU L, 15-24 Oct. 21 at Wisconsin W, 42-0 Oct. 28 Minnesota W, 42-10 Nov. 4 at Iowa W, 34-0 Nov. 11 at NW W, 59-14 Nov. 18 Purdue W, 24-6 Nov. 25 at Ohio State W, 14-3 *Jan. 1 USC L, 10-17 *Rose Bowl, Pasadena, California	Sept. 8 NW W, 49-7 Sept. 15 ND L, 10-12 Sept. 22 Kansas W, 28-7 Sept. 29 at Cal. W, 14-10 Oct. 6 at MSU W, 21-7 Oct. 13 Minnesota W, 31-21 Oct. 20 at Illinois W, 27-7 Oct. 27 Indiana W, 27-21 Nov. 3 Wisconsin W, 54-0 Nov. 10 at Purdue L, 21-24 Nov. 17 Ohio State L, 15-18 *Dec. 28 No. Carol. L, 15-17 *Gator Bowl, Jacksonville, Florida	Sept. 13 NW W, 17-10 Sept. 20 at ND L, 27-29 Sept. 27 S. Carolina L, 14-17 Oct. 4 California W, 38-13 Oct. 11 MSU W, 27-23 Oct. 18 at Minnesota W, 37-14 Oct. 25 Illinois W, 45-14 Nov. 1 at Indiana W, 35-0 Nov. 8 at Wisconsin W, 24-0 Nov. 15 Purdue W, 26-0 Nov. 22 at Ohio State W, 9-3 *Jan. 1 Washington W, 23-6 *Rose Bowl, Pasadena, California

1981	1982 **Big Ten Champions**	1983	1984
Coach: Glenn E. "Bo" Schembechler	**Coach:** Glenn E. "Bo" Schembechler	**Coach:** Glenn E. "Bo" Schembechler	**Coach:** Glenn E. "Bo" Schembechler
Season Record: 9-3	**Season Record:** 8-4	**Season Record:** 9-3	**Season Record:** 6-6
Conference Record: 6-3 (3rd Place tie)	**Conference Record:** 8-1 (1st Place)	**Conference Record:** 8-1 (2nd Place)	**Conference Record:** 5-4 (6th Place tie)
Sept. 12 at Wisconsin L, 14-21 Sept. 19 ND W, 25-7 Sept. 26 Navy W, 21-16 Oct. 3 at Indiana W, 38-17 Oct. 10 at MSU W, 38-20 Oct. 17 Iowa L, 7-9 Oct. 24 NW W, 38-0 Oct. 31 at Minnesota W, 34-13 Nov. 7 Illinois W, 70-21 Nov. 14 at Purdue W, 28-10 Nov. 21 Ohio State L, 9-14 *Dec. 31 UCLA W, 33-14 *Bluebonnet Bowl, Houston, Texas	Sept. 11 Wisconsin W, 20-9 Sept. 18 at ND L, 17-23 Sept. 25 UCLA L, 27-31 Oct. 2 Indiana W, 24-10 Oct. 9 MSU W, 31-17 Oct. 16 at Iowa W, 29-7 Oct. 23 at NW W, 49-14 Oct. 30 Minnesota W, 52-14 Nov. 6 at Illinois W, 16-10 Nov. 13 Purdue W, 52-21 Nov. 20 at Ohio State L, 14-24 *Jan. 1 UCLA L, 14-24 *Rose Bowl, Pasadena, California	Sept. 10 Wash. State W, 20-17 Sept. 17 at Wash. L, 24-25. Sept. 24 at Wisc. W, 38-21 Oct. 1 Indiana W, 43-18 Oct. 8 at MSU W, 42-0 Oct. 15 NW W, 35-0 Oct. 22 Iowa W, 16-13 Oct. 29 at Illinois L, 6-16 Nov. 5 Purdue W, 42-10 Nov. 12 at Minn. W, 58-10 Nov. 19 Ohio State W, 24-21 *Jan. 2 Auburn L, 7-9 *Sugar Bowl, New Orleans, Louisiana	Sept. 8 Miami (Fla.) W, 22-14 Sept. 15 Washington L, 11-20 Sept. 22 Wisconsin W, 20-14 Sept. 29 at Indiana W, 14-6 Oct. 6 MSU L, 7-19 Oct. 13 NW W, 31-0 Oct. 20 at Iowa L, 0-26 Oct. 27 Illinois W, 26-18 Nov. 3 at Purdue L, 29-31 Nov. 10 Minnesota W, 31-7 Nov. 17 at Ohio State L, 6-21 *Dec. 21 Brig. Young L, 17-24 *Holiday Bowl, San Diego, California

1985	1986 **Big Ten Champions**	1987	1988 **Big Ten Champions**
Coach: Glenn E. "Bo" Schembechler	**Coach:** Glenn E. "Bo" Schembechler	**Coach:** Glenn E. "Bo" Schembechler	**Coach:** Glenn E. "Bo" Schembechler
Season Record: 10-1-1	**Season Record:** 11-2	**Season Record:** 8-4	**Season Record:** 9-2-1
Conference Record: 6-1-1 (2nd Place)	**Conference Record:** 7-1 (1st Place tie)	**Conference Record:** 5-3 (4th Place)	**Conference Record:** 7-0-1 (1st Place)
Sept. 14 ND W, 20-12 Sept. 21 at S. Carolina W, 34-3 Sept. 28 Maryland W, 20-0 Oct. 5 Wisconsin W, 33-6 Oct. 12 at MSU W, 31-0 Oct. 19 at Iowa L, 10-12 Oct. 26 Indiana W, 42-15 Nov. 2 at Illinois T, 3-3 Nov. 9 Purdue W, 47-0 Nov. 16 at Minnesota W, 48-7 Nov. 23 Ohio State W, 27-17 *Jan. 1 Nebraska W, 27-23 *Fiesta Bowl, Tempe, Arizona	Sept. 13 at ND W, 24-23 Sept. 20 Oregon St. W, 31-12 Sept. 27 Florida St. W, 20-18 Oct. 4 at Wisconsin W, 34-17 Oct. 11 MSU W, 27-6 Oct. 18 Iowa W, 20-17 Oct. 25 at Indiana W, 38-14 Nov. 1 Illinois W, 69-13 Nov. 8 at Purdue W, 31-7 Nov. 15 Minnesota L, 17-20 Nov. 22 at OSU W, 26-24 Dec. 6 at Hawaii W, 27-10 *Jan. 1 Arizona State L, 15-22 *Rose Bowl, Pasadena, California	Sept. 12 ND L, 7-26 Sept. 19 Wash. State W, 44-18 Sept. 26 Long Bch. St. W, 49-0 Oct. 3 Wisconsin W, 49-0 Oct. 10 at MSU L, 11-17 Oct. 17 Iowa W, 37-10 Oct. 24 at Indiana L, 10-14 Oct. 31 NW, W 29-6 Nov. 7 at Minnesota W, 30-20 Nov. 14 at Illinois W, 17-14 Nov. 21 Ohio State L, 20-23 *Jan. 2 Alabama W, 28-24 *Hall of Fame Bowl, Tampa, Florida	Sept. 10 at ND L, 17-19 Sept. 17 Miami (Fla.) L, 30-31 Sept. 24 Wake Forest W, 19-9 Oct. 1 at Wisconsin W, 62-14 Oct. 8 MSU W, 17-3 Oct. 15 at Iowa T, 17-17 Oct. 22 Indiana W, 31-6 Oct. 29 at NW W, 52-7 Nov. 5 Minnesota W, 22-7 Nov. 12 Illinois W, 38-9 Nov. 19 at OSU W, 34-31 *Jan. 2 USC W, 22-14 * Rose Bowl, Pasadena, California

1989 **Big Ten Champions**	1990 **Big Ten Champions**	1991 **Big Ten Champions**	1992 **Big Ten Champions**
Coach: Glenn E. "Bo" Schembechler	**Coach:** Gary O. Moeller	**Coach:** Gary O. Moeller	**Coach:** Gary O. Moeller
Season Record: 10-2	**Season Record:** 9-3	**Season Record:** 10-2	**Season Record:** 9-0-3
Conference Record: 8-0 (1st Place)	**Conference Record:** 6-2 (1st Place tie)	**Conference Record:** 8-0 (1st Place)	**Conference Record:** 6-0-2 (1st Place)
Sept. 16 ND L, 19-24 Sept. 23 at UCLA W, 24-23 Sept. 30 Maryland W, 41-21 Oct. 7 Wisconsin W, 24-0 Oct. 14 at MSU W, 10-7 Oct. 21 at Iowa W, 26-12 Oct. 28 Indiana W, 38-10 Nov. 4 Purdue W, 42-27 Nov. 11 at Illinois W, 24-10 Nov. 18 at Minn. W, 49-15 Nov. 25 Ohio State W, 28-18 *Jan. 1 USC L, 10-17 *Rose Bowl, Pasadena, California	Sept. 15 at ND L, 24-28 Sept. 22 UCLA W, 38-15 Sept. 29 Maryland W, 45-17 Oct. 6 at Wisconsin W, 41-3 Oct. 13 MSU L, 27-28 Oct. 20 Iowa L, 23-24 Oct. 27 at Indiana W, 45-19 Nov. 3 at Purdue W, 38-13 Nov. 10 Illinois W, 22-17 Nov. 17 Minnesota W, 35-18 Nov. 24 at OSU W, 16-13 *Jan. 1 Mississippi W, 35-3 *Gator Bowl, Jacksonville, Florida	Sept. 7 at BC W, 35-13 Sept. 14 ND W, 24-14 Sept. 28 Florida State L, 31-51 Oct. 5 at Iowa W, 43-24 Oct. 12 at MSU W, 45-28 Oct. 19 Indiana W, 24-16 Oct. 25 at Minnesota W, 52-6 Nov. 2 Purdue W, 42-0 Nov. 9 NW W, 59-14 Nov. 16 at Illinois W, 20-0 Nov. 23 Ohio State W, 31-3 *Jan. 1 Washington L, 14-34 *Rose Bowl, Pasadena, California	Sept. 12 at ND T, 17-17 Sept. 19 Okla. State W, 35-3 Sept. 26 Houston W, 61-7 Oct. 3 Iowa W, 52-28 Oct. 10 MSU W, 35-10 Oct. 17 at Indiana W, 31-3 Oct. 24 Minnesota W, 63-13 Oct. 31 at Purdue W, 24-17 Nov. 7 at NW W, 40-7 Nov. 14 Illinois T, 22-22 Nov. 21 at Ohio State T, 13-13 *Jan. 1 Washington W, 38-31 *Rose Bowl, Pasadena, California

1993	1994	1995	1996
Coach: Gary O. Moeller	**Coach:** Gary O. Moeller	**Coach:** Lloyd Carr	**Coach:** Lloyd Carr
Season Record: 8-4	**Season Record:** 8-4	**Season Record:** 9-4	**Overall Record:** 8-4
Conference Record: 5-3 (4th Place tie)	**Conference Record:** 5-3 (3rd Place)	**Conference Record:** 5-3 (3rd Place tie)	**Conference Record:** 5-3 (5th place tie)
Sept. 4 Wash. State W, 41-14 Sept. 11 ND L, 23-27 Sept. 25 Houston W, 42-21 Oct. 2 Iowa W, 24-7 Oct. 9 at MSU L, 7-17 Oct. 16 at PSU W, 21-13 Oct. 23 Illinois L, 21-24 Oct. 30 at Wisconsin L, 10-13 Nov. 6 Purdue W, 25-10 Nov. 13 at Minnesota W, 58-7 Nov. 20 Ohio State W, 28-0 *Jan. 1 NC State W, 42-7 *Hall of Fame Bowl, Tampa, Florida	Sept. 3 BC W, 34-26 Sept. 10 at ND W, 26-24 Sept. 24 Colorado L, 26-27 Oct. 1 at Iowa W, 29-14 Oct. 8 MSU W, 40-20 Oct. 15 Penn State L, 24-31 Oct. 22 at Illinois W, 19-14 Oct. 29 Wisconsin L, 19-31 Nov. 5 at Purdue W, 45-23 Nov. 12 Minnesota W, 38-22 Nov. 19 at Ohio State L, 6-22 *Dec. 30 Colo. State W, 24-14 * Holiday Bowl, San Diego, California	Aug. 26 Virginia W, 18-17 Sept. 2 at Illinois W, 38-14 Sept. 9 Memphis W, 24-7 Sept. 16 at BC W, 23-13 Sept. 30 Miami (OH) W, 38-19 Oct. 7 NW L, 13-19 Oct. 21 at Indiana W, 34-17 Oct. 28 Minnesota W, 52-17 Nov. 4 at MSU L, 25-28 Nov. 11 Purdue W, 5-0 Nov. 18 at Penn State L, 17-27 Nov. 25 Ohio State W, 31-23 *Dec. 28 Texas A&M L, 20-22 *Alamo Bowl, San Antonio, Texas NOTE: Lloyd Carr entered the 1995 season as interim head coach and was named to the job permanently on Nov. 13, 1995.	Aug. 31 Illinois W, 20-8 Sept. 14 at Colorado W, 20-13 Sept. 21 BC W, 20-14 Sept. 28 UCLA W, 38-9 Oct. 5 at NW L, 16-17 Oct. 19 Indiana W, 27-20 Oct. 26 at Minnesota W, 44-10 Nov. 2 MSU W, 45-29 Nov. 9 at Purdue L, 3-9 Nov. 16 Penn State L, 17-29 Nov. 23 at Ohio State W, 13-9 *Jan. 1 Alabama L, 14-17 *Outback Bowl, Tampa, Florida

1997 **Big Ten Champions, National Champions**	1998 **Big Ten Champions**	1999	2000 **Big Ten Champions**
Coach: Lloyd Carr	**Coach:** Lloyd Carr	**Coach:** Lloyd Carr	**Coach:** Lloyd Carr
Overall Record: 12-0	**Overall Record:** 10-3	**Overall Record:** 10-2	**Overall Record:** 9-3
Conference Record: 8-0 (1st Place)	**Conference Record:** 7-1 (1st Place tie)	**Conference Record:** 6-2 (2nd Place tie)	**Conference Record:** 6-2 (1st Place tie)
Sept. 13 Colorado W, 27-3 Sept. 20 Baylor W, 38-3 Sept. 27 ND W, 21-14 Oct. 4 at Indiana W, 37-0 Oct. 11 NW W, 23-6 Oct. 18 Iowa W, 28-24 Oct. 25 at MSU W, 23-7 Nov. 1 Minnesota W, 24-3 Nov. 8 at Penn State W, 34-8 Nov. 15 at Wisconsin W, 26-16 Nov. 22 Ohio State W, 20-14 *Jan. 1 Wash. St. W, 21-16 * Rose Bowl, Pasadena, California	Sept. 5 at ND L, 20-36 Sept. 12 Syracuse L, 28-38 Sept. 19 EMU W, 59-20 Sept. 26 MSU W, 29-17 Oct. 3 at Iowa W, 12-9 Oct. 17 at NW W, 12-6 Oct. 24 Indiana W, 21-10 Oct. 31 at Minnesota W, 15-10 Nov. 7 Penn State W, 27-0 Nov. 14 Wisconsin W, 27-10 Nov. 21 OSU L, 16-31 Nov. 28 at Hawaii W, 48-17 *Jan. 1 Arkansas W, 45-31 *CompUSA Florida Citrus Bowl, Orlando, Florida	Sept. 4 ND W, 26-22 Sept. 11 Rice W, 37-3 Sept. 18 at Syracuse W, 18-13 Sept. 25 at Wisc. W, 21-16 Oct. 2 Purdue W, 38-12 Oct. 9 at MSU L, 31-34 Oct. 23 Illinois L, 29-35 Oct. 30 at Indiana W, 34-31 Nov. 6 NW W, 37-3 Nov. 13 at PSU W, 31-27 Nov. 20 Ohio State W, 24-17 *Jan. 1 Alabama W, 35-34 OT *FedEx Orange Bowl, Miami, Florida	Sept. 2 Bowl. Green W, 42-7 Sept. 9 Rice W, 38-7 Sept. 16 at UCLA L, 20-23 Sept. 23 at Illinois W, 35-31 Sept. 30 Wisconsin W, 13-10 Oct. 7 at Purdue L, 31-32 Oct. 14 Indiana W, 58-0 Oct. 21 MSU W, 14-0 Nov. 4 at NW L, 51-54 Nov. 11 Penn State W, 33-11 Nov. 18 at OSU W, 38-26 *Jan. 1 Auburn W, 31-28 *CompUSA Florida Citrus Bowl, Orlando, Florida

67

2001	2002	2003 **Big Ten Champions**	2004 **Big Ten Champions**
Coach: Lloyd Carr	**Coach:** Lloyd Carr	**Coach:** Lloyd Carr	**Coach:** Lloyd Carr
Overall Record: 8-4	**Overall Record:** 10-3	**Overall Record:** 10-3	**Overall Record:** 9-3
Conference Record: 6-2 (2nd Place)	**Conference Record:** 6-2 (3rd Place)	**Conference Record:** 7-1 (1st Place)	**Conference Record:** 7-1 (1st Place tie)
Sept. 1 Miami (Ohio) W, 31-13 Sept. 8 at Wash. L, 18-23 Sept. 22 WMU W, 38-21 Sept. 29 Illinois W, 45-20 Oct. 6 at Penn State W, 20-0 Oct. 13 Purdue W, 24-10 Oct. 27 at Iowa W, 32-26 Nov. 3 at MSU L, 24-26 Nov. 10 Minnesota W, 31-10 Nov. 17 at Wisconsin W, 20-17 Nov. 24 Ohio State L, 20-26 *Jan. 1 Tennessee L, 17-45 *Capital One Florida Citrus Bowl, Orlando, Florida	Aug. 31 Washington W, 31-29 Sept. 7 WMU W, 35-12 Sept. 14 at ND L, 23-25 Sept. 21 Utah W, 10-7 Sept. 28 at Illinois W, 45-28 Oct. 12 PSU W, 27-24 OT Oct. 19 at Purdue W, 23-21 Oct. 26 Iowa L, 9-34 Nov. 2 MSU W, 49-3 Nov. 9 at Minnesota W, 41-24 Nov. 16 Wisconsin W, 21-14 Nov. 23 at Ohio State L, 9-14. *Jan. 1 Florida W, 38-30 * Outback Bowl, Tampa, Florida	Aug. 30 CMU W, 45-7 Sept. 6 Houston W, 50-3 Sept. 13 ND W, 38-0 Sept. 20 at Oregon L, 27-31 Sept. 27 Indiana W, 31-17 Oct. 4 at Iowa L, 27-30 Oct. 10 at Minnesota W, 38-35 Oct. 18 Illinois W, 56-14 Oct. 25 Purdue W, 31-3 Nov. 1 at MSU W, 27-20 Nov. 15 at NW W, 41-10 Nov. 22 Ohio State W, 35-21 *Jan. 1 USC L, 14-28 * Rose Bowl, Pasadena, Calif.	Sept. 4 Miami (Ohio) W, 43-10 Sept. 11 at ND L, 20-28 Sept. 18 S. Diego St. W, 24-21 Sept. 25 Iowa W, 30-17 Oct. 2 at Indiana W, 35-14 Oct. 9 Minnesota W, 27-24 Oct. 16 at Illinois W, 30-19 Oct. 23 at Purdue W, 16-14 Oct. 30 MSU W, 45-37 OT Nov. 13 NW W, 42-20 Nov. 20 at Ohio State L, 21-37 *Jan. 1 Texas L, 37-38 *Rose Bowl, Pasadena, California

2005	2006	2007	2008
Coach: Lloyd Carr	**Coach:** Lloyd Carr	**Coach:** Lloyd Carr	**Coach:** Rich Rodriguez
Overall Record: 7-5	**Overall Record:** 11-2	**Overall Record:** 9-4	**Overall Record:** 3-9
Conference Record: 5-3 (3rd Place tie)	**Conference Record:** 7-1 (2nd Place tie)	**Conference Record:** 6-2 (2nd Place tie)	**Conference Record:** 2-6 (9th Place tie)
Sept. 3 No. Illinois W, 33-17 Sept. 10 ND L, 10-17 Sept. 17 EMU W, 55-0 Sept. 24 at Wisconsin L, 20-23 Oct. 1 at MSU W, 34-31 OT Oct. 8 Minnesota L, 20-23 Oct. 15 Penn State W, 27-25 Oct. 22 at Iowa W, 23-20 OT Oct. 29 at NW W, 33-17 Nov. 12 Indiana W, 41-14 Nov. 19 Ohio State L, 21-25 *Dec. 28 Nebraska L, 28-32 * Alamo Bowl, San Antonio, Texas	Sept. 2 Vanderbilt W, 27-7 Sept. 9 CMU W, 41-17 Sept. 16 at ND W, 47-21 Sept. 23 Wisconsin W, 27-13 Sept. 30 at Minnesota W, 28-14 Oct. 7 MSU W, 31-13 Oct. 14 at Penn State W, 17-10 Oct. 21 Iowa W, 20-6 Oct. 28 NW W, 17-3 Nov. 4 Ball State W, 34-26 Nov. 11 at Indiana W, 34-3 Nov. 18 at Ohio State L, 39-42 * Jan. 1 USC L, 18-32 * Rose Bowl, Pasadena, California	Sept. 1 App. State L, 32-34 Sept. 8 Oregon L, 7-39 Sept. 15 ND W, 38-0 Sept. 22 Penn State W, 14-9 Sept. 29 at NW W, 28-16 Oct. 6 EMU W, 33-22 Oct. 13 Purdue W, 48-21 Oct. 20 at Illinois W, 27-17 Oct. 27 Minnesota W, 34-10 Nov. 3 at MSU W, 28-24 Nov. 10 at Wisconsin L, 21-37 Nov. 17 Ohio State L, 3-14 *Jan. 1 Florida W, 41-35 *Capital One Bowl, Orlando, Florida	Aug. 30 Utah L, 23-25 Sept. 6 Miami (Ohio) W, 16-6 Sept. 13 at ND L, 17-35 Sept. 27 Wisconsin W, 27-25 Oct. 4 Illinois (HC) L, 20-45 Oct. 11 Toledo L, 10-13 Oct. 18 at Penn State L, 17-46 Oct. 25 MSU L, 21-35 Nov. 1 at Purdue L, 42-48 Nov. 8 at Minnesota W, 29-6 Nov. 15 NW L, 14-21 Nov. 22 at Ohio State L, 7-42

The following individuals/institutions are acknowledged for granting permission to use photos:

Joseph Arcure: photos of Bo Schembechler on players' shoulders (B); Anthony Carter (O); hand holding up winged helmet (W).

Bentley Historical Library: photos of Michigan Stadium/Crisler Arena (A); Gerald Ford in football uniform (F); Desmond Howard's Heisman pose (H); 1969 UM football team (L); UM-MSU lined up over the ball (P); Bob Ufer (U); Fielding Yost with players (Y); 1901 Rose Bowl team (Z).

Per Kjeldsen: photos of M flag (C); B.J. Askew's diving touchdown (E); defensive play vs. OSU (G); Jon Jansen with Little Brown Jug (J); Remy Hamilton's kick vs. ND (K); 1997 National championship composite (N); Brian Griese (Q); Charles Woodson with a rose (R); Michigan Stadium at sunset (S); UM drum major (V); Lloyd Carr with players (X).

Wolverine Photo: photos of Mike Hart (D) (by Amir Gamzu); players in huddle (I) (by Amir Gamzu); football field (M) (by Jonathan LeFaive); players in tunnel (T) (by Jonathan LeFaive).